LAWRENCE GROBEL'S BOOKS

CONVERSATIONS WITH CAPOTE: "A wonderfully outrageous read. The most entertaining glitz of the season."–*The Denver Post.*

CONVERSATIONS WITH BRANDO: "You got me!" –Marlon Brando

AL PACINO In Conversation with Lawrence Grobel: "Journalist Grobel, who literally wrote the book on interviewing, puts his talents on full display... Part of the book's draw is witnessing the two become closer as the years go by...making for increasingly engaging and illuminating reading."–*Publisher's Weekly* Starred Review

CLIMBING HIGHER (for Montel Williams): "An absolutely riveting read."–*N. Y. Post.* "I would recommend Larry Grobel as a therapist to just about anybody." –Montel Williams

THE ART OF THE INTERVIEW: Lessons from a Master of the Craft: "Grobel gives readers the equivalent of a master class in this thoroughly entertaining treatise on one of the toughest tasks in journalism.... The book also satisfies the voyeuristic desires of a celebrity obsessed culture by raising the curtain on the idiosyncratic demands of stars."–*Publisher's Weekly*

Also by Lawrence Grobel

Fiction

Begin Again Finnegan

Catch a Fallen Star

The Black Eyes of Akbah

Commando Ex

Memoir

You Show Me Yours

Nonfiction

Conversations with Ava Gardner

Signing In: 50 Celebrity Profiles

"I Want You in My Movie!" The Making of Al Pacino's WildeSalome

Yoga? No! Shmoga!

Marilyn & Me (for Lawrence Schiller)

Icons: 15 Celebrity Profiles

Al Pacino: In Conversation with Lawrence Grobel

Conversations with Robert Evans

The Art of the Interview: Lessons from a Master of the Craft

Climbing Higher (with Montel Williams)

Endangered Species: Writers Talk About Their Craft, Their Vision, Their Lives

Above the Line: Conversations About the Movies

Conversations with Michener

The Hustons

Conversations with Brando

Conversations with Capote

Madonna Paints a Mustache

a Mustache

& Other Celebrity Encounters

Lawrence Grobel

FIRST EDITION

Copyright © 2014 Lawrence Grobel

Cover Design: Roberta Grobel Intrater

Illustration Maria Eugenia Ortega, from a photograph by Alberto Tolot, used with permission

Back Cover: Paul Singer

Back cover photos taken by Harvey Wang, Lori Stoll, Alberto Tolot, Hiromi Grobel, & Larry Grobel courtesy of Lawrence Grobel

www.lawrencegrobel.com

ISBN-10: 1502327902
ISBN-13: 9781502327901

For Elliott Gould
Who challenged me to go
Beyond "Information"

Come, partake of my poetry salad
Tossed with haikus, quatrains,
  odes and ballads
There'll be rhymes, couplets,
  and tasty blank verses
Just hope my subjects won't
  be sending me curses
Because I'm not flattering,
  cloying or sweet
Even though I may have
  some words to eat

Contents

Introduction

Though the poems in this book are about very pub-lic, very private people, they are also very personal. After spending time interviewing a particular subject for a book or magazine article, I often found myself thinking about a specific detail that seemed to define that person for me. Occasionally I'd jot down a few lines at the time; more often it was a few years later. That's when I knew there must be some truth to these observations—they had passed the test of time, and they often made me smile.

Celebrities allow for fantasies. We fall in love with them, and then root for their downfall. We worship their beauty and talent, and then quietly applaud their public disintegration. We know they are richer than we are, live in bigger homes, drive better cars, have a bountiful range of sexual exploration, but we aren't quite willing to consider them smarter or better read or more friends-and-family inclined that we are. They exist not just for themselves, but for us. And once in a while we're given entry into their inner sanctums, their private islands, their touring buses, their back-yards, bedrooms, or swimming pools. It may only be temporary, but then, so are they.

It all began in the early 1970s, when my editor at *Newsday* assigned me to interview "Household Names," beginning with Mae West. I continued doing interviews, but on a deeper level, when I started writing for *Playboy* in 1976, with Barbra Streisand as my first subject. I did about 50 *Playboy* interviews, which brought me into the lives of some very famous people for extended periods of time. I also wrote for other magazines, like *Rolling Stone, Movieline, Reader's Digest, Redbook* and *The Saturday Evening Post.* When Playboy Cable TV wanted to duplicate their famous interviews on the air, they asked me to give it a try, and I did another 50 for them with two cameras filming us.

These poems are often the result of one particular moment in my encounters with these "Household Names." The one about Lauren Bacall, for instance, happened when I first met her in the living room of her New York apartment. With Lucille Ball, the inspiration came when she told me that she was ready to die, since most of her friends were gone. Marlon Brando's bet made me uncomfortable. Jake Gyllenhaal's publicist was the spark for what I wrote about my limited interview time. The same with Barbara Walters' publicist, who interrupted my talk with Walters. Ava Gardner told me a touching story about her childhood. Madonna said something to my daughter I never forgot. Pavarotti took off his shirt in my living room and I knew I had something. Olivia de Havilland's tears surprised me. My phone call to Bette Davis turned very long distance, and Bette Midler's call to me was puzzling. Seeing

Barbra Streisand in Malibu was a glimpse into her being a perfectionist. Kiefer Sutherland actually lassoed me. Al Pacino was handy with a broom. Christopher Walken cleaned countertops. These were the kinds of moments on which I zeroed in.

Though some of these poems are about celebrities who are no longer with us, or whose lives have had some dramatic changes, I've tried to capture a particular moment in time. They are private glimpses into their rarified air. True, they breathe the same smog and suffer from the decline of ozone protection as the rest of us, but somehow we suspect that they don't button their clothes the way we do. They do, of course. But that doesn't mean we have to believe it.

CHILDHOOD

AVA GARDNER'S DOLL

Ava Gardner had a doll;
She lost it in the rain
Her father wouldn't let her
Look for it
Young Ava was never the same

.

KIM BASINGER THREE YEARS OLD

When Kim Basinger's daddy
Took her to school when
She was three years old
She thought that four-hour day
Was school
And cried when told she had to
Return
For thirteen more years

ANTHONY KIEDIS FILM STAR

Anthony Kiedis's first director
Was his film school father
Who instructed him to
Hit a homeless man
Over the head
And steal his wallet

The 4-year-old would grow up
To become a rock star
His dad the president
Of his fan club

MELANIE GRIFFITH GREW UP

Melanie Griffith grew up
With lions on her bed
An abusive stepfather
And a toy coffin
Alfred Hitchcock had given her

CLARABELL POINTED TO ME

Clarabell pointed to me
Buffalo Bob signaled
Come on down
From the Peanut Gallery
But it was the Seltzer-spritzing
Clown, so much scarier in color
That kept me from saying
Howdy to my Doody hero

KURT RUSSELL CHASED MICKEY MANTLE

Kurt Russell chased Mickey Mantle's
Car in the Stadium lot
Sticking out his hand
Hoping for a signed ball
The Mick rolled up his window
On the 8-year-old's arm
And taught Kurt a lesson
He's never forgot
Don't ask Kurt Russell for
His autograph

LILY TOMLIN NEVER MET SMOKEY THE BEAR

Lily Tomlin once burned down
a barn
and never told anyone

MORGAN FAIRCHILD WASN'T A BAD CHILD

Morgan Fairchild wasn't a bad child
But claims nine of the ten worst
Things that could happen
Growing up
Happened
Proving once again
You don't just play a bitch
You earn it

LESLEY-ANN WARREN GREW BIG BREASTS

Lesley-Ann Warren grew big breasts
Very young,
Dreamed of giant penises,
And was afraid

FREDDIE PRINZE JR. SUPERHERO

Freddie Prinze Jr. played
In a superhero world
To replace his dad
Who killed himself at 22.
When a high school bully
Pushed him down at a party
Freddie turned into his superhero.
"I kept hitting that kid until
His face wasn't hard any more."
When he walked away
No one laughed at him
Even when he cried

ANJELICA HUSTON CASTS HER SHADOW

Anjelica Huston wanted me
Off the set of *The Dead*
Because every time she
Looked at me
She saw her mother
Who died in a car crash
When Anjelica was 16
And things between them
Were unresolved

BRENDAN FRASER WENT
TO PREP SCHOOL

Brendan Fraser went to prep school
In Toronto. How cruel?
He was pulled from his bed
A pillow case over his head
Thrown in the trunk of a car
And driven kind of far
Where he was left
Somewhat bereft
Shirtless and feeling the fool
Tied at a playground near the local girl's school.
It certainly sounds kind of crummy
But remember, he grew up to star in *The Mummy*

ASHLEY JUDD SPITS TOBACCO

Ashley Judd's first kiss
Came in the first grade.
She attended 12 schools
In 13 years
As her distant father advised her
To go easy on the boys
Because "You've got something
We don't."
In *The Locusts* her character
Was called a *cum-bucket*.
"One of the most searing insults
I've ever heard."
She believes ponytails and
Water are the keys to
Happiness
Chews tobacco
Which she spits
Into a Cinderella cup
From Disneyland

FAMILY

WHEN HALLE BERRY THINKS OF HER FATHER

When Halle Berry thinks of her father
What she sees is the toy Maltese
Flying across the dining room.
"My father was abusive."
And ever since
She's been trying to find
The right man

JAMIE LEE

Jamie Lee Curtis
Had no problems with
Janet Leigh
But thinks her father
Tony
Was a ghost

MARILYN CHAMBERS SHUTS THE GREEN DOOR

Marilyn Chambers shuts the green door
And shudders at the thought of
Her father taking in her movie
Without being told he was
About to see
His little girl
Suddenly
All grown up

DON'T FEEL SORRY
FOR SALLY FIELD

Don't feel sorry for Sally Field
Who's never had friends
Other than anger.
When she throws a tantrum now
Her son tells her
To go to her room
And she obeys

ROBIN WILLIAMS SHOOTING PLANES

Robin Williams sat at his
Computer shooting at planes
While his son stood behind him
Quietly waiting his turn

HARRISON CAN AF-FORD HIS SECRETS

Fugitive witness Harrison Ford
Presumed himself innocent
Of playing patriot games
When he cracked his whip
As Indiana Jones
And flew among galaxies
In the wars between stars

When he sits for publicity
He expects full complicity
With those who'd like to pull
Him out

With nothing personal to reveal
He backs into his dad's hatred
Of his own father
Who took to booze
Blackface theatricals
And died at 25

Little was said of that family
History
And now Harrison can afford
Not to let it hang him up in public

Unlike the scar on his chin
His hurts are in places
We can't see

HANK FONDA HAS TO PEE

Henry Fonda pale and weak
Says he's got to pee
And calls for Shirley.

He remembers his father taking him
To a lynching;
And how his own son Peter
Told the press
That he had once been crucified against a
Chain linked fence.
"Peter is a fucking liar," Henry says,
Shaking the last drops
Onto his pajamas

I KINDA WONDA BRIDGET FONDA

I kinda wonda Bridget Fonda
Why you never really talked ta
Your Aunt Jane
When it's plain as the thinness
Of your upper lip
That journalists
Will want to know of that relation-
ship.
You have little insight into
Grandpa Henry,
Though correctly place father Peter
As the child to your (wo)man.
On screen you are perhaps the freest
Fonda, revealing and uninhibited.
Conversationally though, you're still
Kinda limited

JAMES GARNER, ALMOST MURDERER

When James Garner was 13
He nearly choked his stepmother
To death.
"I can understand how kids
Can rebel to the point of murder,"
He said, describing how she humiliated
Him time and again
Making him wear a dress
As his brothers called him Louise.
"Wilma was a nasty bitch. She
Used to beat the hell out of me."
She gave him one last whupping
After his dad and brother pulled him
Off her as she gagged.
But it was worth it
Because that broke up their
Miserable marriage

HOW OLIVER STONE CHOOSES
HIS SUBJECTS

Oliver Stone's father
Locked his mother
Out of their house
When he was 14 and in boarding school.
She moved to France
Without telling him
Sending him into therapy.
After the divorce she brought him
To a nudist colony in Europe
To explain what happened.

When Oliver returned from
Vietnam
He slipped a tab of acid
Into his father's Scotch
At a party in the Hamptons.
His dad went to hug a tree
Asking at dinner
"Who's the Judas
At the table?"

DREW BARRYMORE KEEPS HER
FIRST GRAY HAIR

Drew Barrymore keeps her first gray hair
In a plastic bag, duly labeled.
"Every time I get my heart broken," she says,
"I think that love doesn't exist."

The Barrymores, she says,
Were all very, very crazy.
She feels closest to Grandfather John
Whose friends snuck his dead body
To Errol Flynn's house
For a proper send-off.
"I hope to God," Drew says,
"My friends steal my body
Out of a morgue and throw a party
When I'm dead"

RELATIONSHIPS

OLIVIA DE HAVILLAND CRIED

Olivia de Havilland cried
When she remembered back
A half century
To an engagement that never
Went to vows
And the director John Huston
She couldn't
Forget

MERYL STREEP IS VERY DEEP

Meryl Streep is very deep,
Learns her lines in her sleep;
Lost two men to drugs and disease,
Now Meryl does just what she pleases

CHARLIE SHEEN'S GIRLFRIEND

Charlie Sheen's girlfriend
Shot a piece of the toilet
Into her flesh
When she shook Charlie's
Dirty jeans before laundering
And his gun fell out firing

GEE, DAVID DUCHOVNY
[before the divorce]

Gee, David Duchovny
Reading your love poetry
About the lovely Leoni
And your marriage
Gamophobia
`

You have looked love in the face
And felt somethin' thumpin'
Your heart jumpin'

Unless I'm reading your love song
Wrong
And this is about some earlier romance
Perhaps that youthful fling
When you were sixteen

Or some opium dream
But this seems no half-hearted ka-ching!

You're Chagall flying
Not X-designing
You're Henry Jamesian,
Molly Bloomian
Saying yes yes yes
To the Real Thing

NICOLE KIDMAN BROUGHT SUSHI

Nicole Kidman feeling so free
First time we met brought sushi
She didn't forget
Her Down-Under manners
Sushi better than bananas

I stared at her skin
Smooth porcelain
And in dim light
Marveled at her height
(My daughters came to see
She was taller than me)

As a kid she read *Lady Chatterley's Lover*
Saw modern dance with men uncovered
Watched nursing films about sex
At 12 it didn't seem so complex
Did some Aussie TV, and then was gone
Fell head-over-heels for a guy named Tom
Added two adopted kids to their family
Then lost him to the Spaniard Penelope

Came back strong in *Moulin Rouge*
Showed the world she didn't need Cruise
Then found a country singer named Urban
Now she's in Nashville, being suburban

IN ARTHUR MILLER'S KITCHEN

I waited in Arthur Miller's kitchen
For him to finish with the *Times*
Reporter
Wondering if he would talk about
The decline of his most famous wife
Who, in the hot Nevada desert, had
Slammed a car door in his face
And disappeared
In air-conditioned anger
Leaving him to burn,
Thinking how he had written
This movie for her
And it was all falling apart.
In his Manhattan apartment
These many years later
Arthur Miller sadly said,
"If there was a key to Marilyn's
Despair I did not possess it."
And if he did
She probably would have
Changed the lock

NORMAN MAILER WANTS
TO BE KICKED IN THE HEAD

I'd read Norman Mailer said he'd pay
Five dollars for a provocative question
But his college audience was too respectful
So when I had my shot I led
With the wife-stabbing,
Followed with a combination
On his two weeks in Bellevue
And was he crazy?
When he tugged at his turtleneck and asked
"Why go into these things?"
 I knew I had him reeling.
I misquoted his line
"So long as you use the knife"
Which he corrected, "*A* knife"
Then uppercutted an ex-wife's slash
About his mother being the only true Mrs. Mailer
But Norman left-hooked, "An ex-wife looking
To make a lousy remark and succeeding."
When it was over, he rubbed his jaw
And I gave him the bill.
He said I had earned it

SEX

LUNCH AT THE IVY

At lunch at the Ivy
Near where the carousel music plays
Jeff Bridges tries to remember
All the great John Huston stories
He couldn't wait to tell
But all he comes up with
Is a tour through the Prado
Listening to the old man talk
About Goya and Velasquez
As Bridges' stomach churned
From the poisoned sea food
And the strange Spanish girl
He ate the night before

ROBERT MITCHUM TOLD NICK NOLTE

Robert Mitchum told Nick Nolte
Who told me:
On the set of *My Forbidden Past*
Ava Gardner asked Mitchum
"When are you going to fuck me?"
Mitchum demurred, "Jesus Ava...
I don't know"
And left it that way
Until the next day when Nolte asked
"Did you ever fuck Ava?"
"Oh no," Mitchum replied
"Too addictive"

Nolte was impressed
"One of the greatest compliments
You can give an actress"

SANDRA BULLOCK'S SECRET SEX LIFE

When Sandra Bullock was a waitress
She was attacked by a druggie with a gun
Who dragged her into an alley
Mumbling "Pussy."
"You want pussy it will be a dead pussy
Because you'll have to shoot me," she said,
Turning her back to him
And walking away.

She once kissed a guy where their mouths fit
Together like pieces of a puzzle.
"The sad thing is, you spend
The rest of your life
Looking for it again."

Her naked body went viral
On the Internet
Only it wasn't her.
 "The boobs were
Much better. Big. A nice rack.
But they were not mine."

She likes to wear men's underwear
But doesn't want a guy to wear hers.
She once had a boyfriend though
Who made her laugh
When he wore one on his head

DR. RUTH FELL ASLEEP IN MY CAR

Dr. Ruth fell asleep in my car
After asking me how I met my wife
She awoke halfway between Anaheim
And Los Angeles
Asked me about my children
But nodded off as I spoke
Boring her with family talk
Minus the intimate details
Of how the family got made

EGO

STEVE (YAWN) MARTIN

Steve (yawn) Martin
Turns on his bathtub
Jacuzzi to impress
Al Pacino
Who has one of his own

SID CAESAR KNOWS THE STORY OF HIS LIFE

Sid Caesar knows the story of his life
And would be grateful
If you asked him
To start at
The beginning

JAMES FRANCO WAS PRETTY CRANK-O

James Franco was pretty crank-o
When I asked him questions
He didn't want to answer.
"Nah" was his favorite response.
But when we got to our cars
And I saw his new blue Jag
He rolled down his window
And asked me not to write
About that

RAY BRADBURY SO FULL OF HIMSELF

Ray Bradbury is so full of himself
forgive him
if he has
no room
for you

ONLY WARREN BEATTY KNOWS

Only Warren Beatty knows
what it's like
being Warren Beatty

ONLY ANNETTE BENING KNOWS

Only Annette Bening
(helluva lady)
knows what it's like
taming Warren Beatty

FRANK SINATRA HOLDING COURT

Frank Sinatra was holding court
At Chasen's
While Al Pacino and *his* entourage
Sat at a nearby table.
The women with us all leaned
To get a glimpse of Ol' Blue Eyes.
"He's just a man," Pacino said
Doing his best
Not to strain *his* neck

DR. PAULING'S EGO, I PRESUME

Linus Pauling turned me on
To vitamin scams and
The danger of drugs

He wanted to make sure
I understood that he was
The only person ever
To win two unshared Nobel Prizes

We then shared the same
Men's room
Peeing
In separate urinals

HEIDI HOPES TO SCORE A KNOCKOUT

Heidi Fleiss asked:
Was I the guy with the 900 numbers
Who wouldn't leave her alone?

Heidi Fleiss said:
She was ashamed for the grief
She caused her father.

Heidi Fleiss thought:
Hugh Hefner had serious Alzheimer's and
Robert Evans was a great guy.

Heidi Fleiss refused:
To even consider a book or movie deal
About her life as Hollywood's youngest
Madam.

Heidi Fleiss was selling:
Her pajama line with her first name sewn
Into the pants like Everlast.

Heidi Fleiss knew:
The courts would not be lenient
But

Heidi Fleiss was confident:
Her pajamas would make her
One hundred million dollars.

HENRY MOORE IN ITALY/HENRY LESS IN ENGLAND

Henry Moore sat in his backyard
In Forte dei Marmi
Admiring Millet's drawings
As his assistant in Much Hadam
Builds the massive bronzes
From Moore's maquettes
Believing the world has recognized
The wrong artist

ACTING

ALEC BALDWIN'S CURSE

The curse of the actor,
Alec Baldwin said,
Is that you're always boring
Everybody around you
Because you're trying to make them
Into an
Audience

DYLAN McDERMOTT HAS A THEORY

Dylan McDermott has a theory
About actors
"We're all walking milk cartons
Expiration dates everywhere"

BUD CORT'S HIS HAROLD PAST

Bud Cort's his Harold past
      visiting the Actor's Nursing Home,
      wheeling no-legged Mable King
      to her room, bringing sunflowers
      to her neighbor Gracie, 95,
      thinner than Maude
      but with the same mouth running.

She complains about the light,
      the closed curtains, the male nurse,
      the early bed time,
      but purrs when Bud paints her nails,
      rouges her cheeks, lipsticks her mouth;
      bringing life to the old doll
      who still has nowhere to go
      and wishes she was back in
      her own apartment.

Maude knew when it was time
      to take her leave,
Gracie wants a bigger magnifying glass
      to read.

That's the difference between
        real life and the movie screen.

"Ruth Gordon died at 88," Bud says
"Groucho was 86. This one's 95!"

He thinks about the career he could have had
        realizing that if he doesn't find
        his second act soon
        he'll wind up the youngest SAG member
        at the Actor's Home

Where he'll continue to play Harold
        to so many willing Maudes

CHEVY CHASE REMEMBERS LEE MARVIN

Chevy Chase remembers Lee Marvin
Assessing his life's work as
Having made a lot of shit

When ranking his own work
He comes to the conclusion
That he knows
What Lee Marvin meant

CHRIS O'DONNELL WAS VERY KEEN

Chris O'Donnell was very keen
To work with Kiefer S. and Charlie Sheen
Guys his age without much fear
All starring as *Three Musketeers*

Realized how they were unique
While he was still paying his dues
Seeing Charlie buying "antique
Watches, like I buy tennis shoes"

For the premiere of *Batman Forever*
Said hi to the kids of Henry Winkler
A TV star from *Happy Days* youth
Which brought him to a higher truth

Movies are great, but what made him queasy
Was realizing "My God, it's Fonzie!"

BARBARA HERSHEY STALLED
IN THE FAST LANE

Barbara Hershey admired a friend
Who could talk to anybody.
"He was curious, I wasn't"
Because "shyness is a sweet name
For being self-involved"

In high school she was told
She wasn't old enough to play
Lady Macbeth

Took a midnight rain-soaked drive
On the freeway with four friends
Questioning "Do I really want
To act?"

Got her answer
When the car
Spun three times
And stalled across the fast lane.
She looked at the sky and said
"OK, I'll do it"

On the set of one of her movies
She was still asking
"Is the acting world a phony world
And the crew the real world?"
Remembered that spinning car,
Accepted there are two worlds
Happening simultaneously
And stopped asking questions

DANNY DEVITO DROOLS A LOT

Danny DeVito drools a lot
As Penguin Oswald Cobblepot
(though he doesn't play it
with such glee
as ruthless Sam or *Taxi's* Louie).
He's perfected the art of comic cruel
(a long way from hairdressing
and hustling pool).
As *Cuckoo's* Martini he was
Mentally cracked;
Now he's directing *Hoffa*
Because he stayed friends
With Jack

HOW THE MOVIES DECEIVE

Charlton Heston and I stood
On opposite ends of a
Henry Moore sculpture
Outside the county museum
and nodded,
He acknowledging my recognition,
Me wondering if Moses,
Judah, and Michelangelo
Were really that small

ADVICE

REMEMBER BRAD DOURIF?

Remember Brad Dourif in *Wiseblood*?
How he stuck his face into
The face of fakeblind Harry Dean Stanton?
Brad didn't know how he was
To act throughout that movie
So he shared his discomfort
With us and hated John Huston
For not doing his job.
But Huston liked Dourif's
Teetering on the edge
So much that he just left him
Alone.
A lesson in direction
Not even his actor
Understood

JOHN HUSTON'S ADVICE TO A FIRST TIME NOVELIST

"You don't shake your head yes,
You nod"

NANCY REAGAN'S SECRET SERVICE

Nancy Reagan's Secret Service goon
Eyed me sternly
When I said I'd fight for more time
To hear her childhood memories
Of Uncle Walter Huston
Whom she once counseled
Against singing "September Song"
In *Knickerbocker Holiday.*
So much
For
Just Say No

MADONNA PAINTS A MUSTACHE

Madonna paints a mustache
On her magazine picture,
Wraps her Breathless black fur
Around my 9-year old daughter's shoulders
Then confuses her with advice
"If someone sticks his tongue out
At you, say, *No thanks,*
I use toilet paper"

SILENCE, JODIE FOSTER

Whatzit cost ta
Talk to Jodie Foster?
Very succinctly:
Don't mention Hinckley.
As for sex,
It's too complex.
Just keep it gloss, sir,
When you talk to Jodie Foster

JIM CARREY'S PSYCHIC PHASE

Jim Carrey once went to a psychic
Who told him colors were missing
From his aura
So Carrey went shopping for
Colored ribbons
Before his moment of Zen
When he realized his aura
Would be just fine
Without the ribbons

ASK RICHARD GERE

Ask Richard Gere
What happens when you die?
He'll answer
What happens when you live?
Freudian therapy, he'll say,
Deals with the First Noble Truth:
The Truth of Suffering.
Buddhism goes one better:
The Sense of Transcendence.

Filming *The Cotton Club*
Gere was caught
Pissing in an alley.
"I'm going to have to give you
A summons, Mr Gere," the cop said.
"And by the way, if you
Need any security,
Here's my card"

WESLEY SNIPES SPOKE ABOUT COLOR THEORY

Wesley Snipes spoke about color theory
"Want to study, use more yellow
Want a cooler, open, compassionate
Environment, use blue, turquoise
Or soft green
Want to create more energy, use
White light or some reds."
And if you want to stay out of jail
Pay the IRS

MYSTICISM

MAE WEST WAS QUITE A PEST

Mae West was quite a pest
To nonbelievers who were her guests
At séances, readings, and
Sunday performances
Of her newly discovered
Clairvoyantses

To those who scoffed
That she was really a man,
She flexed her breasts
And didn't give a damn

To her, W.C. Fields was just a loser
(His Little Chickadee hated boozers).
Twice-daily enemas and carrot juice
Were what bonded her
Forty years before Jane Fonda

PATRICK SWAYZE SAVED FROM DROWNING

Patrick Swayze showed me his
Crystals
Spoke of their powers
And swore that a
Ghost saved him from
Drowning
After a wave threw him
From his surfboard

I SAVED AVA'S DNA

Working with Ava Gardner on her memoir
Stories of broken marriages and early film noir
How she outdrank Hemingway, Dominguin, Shaw
and Gable
And danced the flamenco barefoot on Spanish tables

She thought my briefcase kind of a rag
Wanted to get me a new Gucci bag
Said she lived in our canyon in the '40s
Met my daughters and promised them corgis

Didn't ask if we minded her smoke
As she lit up while telling a joke
Left behind a unique amulet
The lipstick'd butt of her cigarette

Could have trashed it, but I knew better
As I helped her numb arm through her sweater
Though she'd had a stroke she was still coquettish
And yes, I've saved that butt—my personal fetish

PARANOIA

STEVE ALLEN HAS AN FBI NUMBER

Steve Allen has an FBI Number
and thinks you should
too

ED ASNER OPENS HIS MAIL

Liberal Ed Asner opens his mail
And talks to strangers
In the safety of his home
Knowing once outside he's
A barrel wide target

PATTY HEARST HUNTS PIGS & DEER

Patty Hearst hunts pigs and deer
Visited the fugitive Shah in Panama
Keeps the *Time* & *Newsweek* covers
Sent by collectors for her signature
Tells me, over sushi–
The diamond in her sheriff's pin
Catching the light–
"I would like to kill
You!"

JERRY LEWIS STICKS A NASA MINI MIC

Jerry Lewis sticks a NASA mini mic
Into his tape recorder and
Snaps pictures of his
Interrogator saying,
"I do this because I've been
Fucked up the ass and I
Don't like it."
He also says his son Gary
Would have been better
Off dead than drugged
In Vietnam
And swings a golf club
In his office, trying to
Par his day

BAD BEHAVIOR

JEWISH GUILT

Robert Mitchum wanted to see me
But didn't want to start talking.
When I said I was there at his request
And was only doing my job
He replied, "That's what Eichmann said."
When he repeated it to make his point
I wondered what poor Jew so
Embittered this man?
And then thought…
Could it be me?

THE BALLAD OF HOWARD & AVA

When Ava Gardner wasn't there
To meet Howard Hughes's plane,
It soon became very clear
When he heard Mickey Rooney's name.

"How dare you!" Howard shouted
And punched her in the eye.
"Howard!" Ava glowered
And let a brass bell fly.

It struck as he yelled "Whore!"
Made him lose a tooth.
He crumbled to the floor,
One-eyed Ava in pursuit.

"I would have killed him," Ava said,
Having lifted a chair above his head.
"Ava!" the maid's voice so tense it
Brought black-eyed Ava to her senses.

THE LOVE SONG OF B. WILLIS

Bruce Willis once lived on my block
Disturbing the peace
By blasting hard rock.
The police were summoned
And took him away;
Then Willis made *Die Hard*
And had the last say.
He married a movie star
And moved out of reach;
Divorced; bought an island
And walks along the beach

WHEN CHRISTIAN SLATER GOT OUT OF JAIL

When Christian Slater got out of jail
He chose me to tell his tale
"I want the press to leave me alone
After I spill my guts to *Rolling Stone*"

He landed there for weird behavior
Resulting from friends who did him no favor
Offering strong drugs & alcohol
To a 29-year-old who couldn't hold it all

Jail was a gift, he said
"I washed cars, made beds
I hated myself, I felt phony,
A fraud, a fake, and often lonely

I couldn't look people in the eye"
Somehow he managed to get by
In the pen he atoned for his sins
As he felt freer than he'd ever been

PIERCE BROSNAN SLIPPED HIS TONGUE

Pierce Brosnan slipped his tongue
and called his groupies
dogs
when compared to his
dead wife

ZSA ZSA AIN'T SO GA-GA

Zsa Zsa ain't so ga-ga
When you look inside her house
And wonder why she
Once eavesdropped on Marilyn
Monroe's hotel doings
Counting the oooh's
Separating the aah's

TONY BENNETT INVITED ME

Tony Bennett invited me to
San Francisco's Fairmont
Where he left his heart
And maybe his mind
Since he didn't remember
I was coming
And had no time

KIEFER SUTHERLAND HAD A ROPE
IN HIS CAR

Kiefer Sutherland had a rope in his car
and when I asked him about the time
he tripped up the script girl by
lassoing both her legs as she walked by
on the set of *The Cowboy Way*, he said
when he snapped the rope to the ground
he was aiming to ensnare just one leg.
A joke, he shrugged, that turned
into an accident.
"Pretty skillful for a city slicker," I said.
"Want to see?" he asked,
picking up the skepticism in my voice.
We went outside where he got the rope
from his trunk,
twirled the loop above his head
and threw it at my feet as I walked
down the street.
He got me
and then gave me the rope.
I've tried it on friends
but haven't come close to
Cowboy Kiefer

BETTE DAVIS PLAYS GARBO

Bette Davis didn't know me
When I called
And before I could explain
She hung up

HOLLYWOOD BABBLE-ON

Farrah Fawcett almost lost her mind
On *Myra Breckinridge* in '69.

Her yellow hair met with protest
By septuagenarian Mae West.
(Of competition she was not fond,
There could be no other blonde.)

Then John Huston behind her appeared
And cupped his hands on her brassiere.

When Racquel Welch saw her smile bright
She said, "Pity your eye teeth aren't as white
As all your others, in fact, they're yellow."

Feline Raquel was a nasty fellow,
As young Farrah from Corpus Christi found out
When during a fitting she heard Welch shout,

"I don't want the slit along the side!"
To which the famed costumer replied,
"It's the forties, that's the look."

But *Myra's* star wouldn't go by the book.
"I want the slit up the front
Like an arrow pointing to my cunt!"

Farrah hadn't heard that word used before
And got a glimpse of what was in store,
Where men became women who were no good.
This was her welcome to Hollywood

DISCOMFORT

TRUMAN CAPOTE SAT BY HIMSELF

Truman Capote sat by himself
At a round table for six at Bobby Van's
I chose my seat, leaving a
Place setting between us
"Well," he chuckled,
Removing the extra knife, fork & spoon,
"I guess we won't need *these*"
I smiled wanly
Knowing he was reading my thoughts
As I made sure there was enough
Space so our legs
Wouldn't touch

JEAN-CLAUDE VAN DAMME &
UNKNOWN FRIEND

Jean-Claude Van Damme
And unknown friend
Called and said, "We're open
to stop by"
It was out of the blue
They had nothing to do
But I had a reason why
It wasn't a good situation
My 16 year-old was having a party
Lots of girls all smiles & perky
And my fatherly intuition
Said no fucking way
I kept Jean-Claude at bay
"Maybe another day"
I told Van Damme
I never heard from him again

JERRY LEE

We had to fly to West Palm Beach
And pay a fee to reach
Jerry Lee
Great Balls of Fire Lewis
Whose whole lot of shakin'
Was apparent as he squirmed
And twisted under the lights
Uncomfortably rehashing
The cradle robbing marriage
The death of wives
The comparisons to Elvis
The family ties to Jimmy Swaggart

His wiry frame and pale demeanor
Was evidence enough
That this hard nosed
Shit kicker
Preferred living
In shadows

NICOLAS CAGE WALKED INTO
A RATTLESNAKE

Nicolas Cage walked into a rattlesnake
While fishing with his cousin Roman
In Napa Valley
When they were teenagers
It was coiled ready to strike
Cage grabbed a pole
With a nail in it
Killed the snake
Brought it home
Removed the poison glands & rattles
And ate it

Years later he found
A baby loon abandoned
At his beach house
And put it in his pool
The loon dove down
"Like God's art"
But the Animal Rescue Agency
Said chlorine was bad for its feathers

Cage brought the loon to
The pet hospital
Where they put it in an
Incubator overnight
Before it died

CHER HEARS THAT A CHILD HAS DIED

Cher hears that a child
has died and
cries guilty tears
because the girl had made her
her last wish
and Cher
was late

IN RFK'S OFFICE

Robert Kennedy had a sailfish
On his wall
A stuffed tiger by the door
And a small black bear near his desk
That sent a chill through my body
When its large wet tongue
Licked my hand
And I realized
It was the Attorney General's dog
And very much alive

RACE

MILES DAVIS DROVE A YELLOW FERRARI

Miles Davis drove a yellow Ferrari,
Thought Jazz meant "nigger,"
And wanted, just once,
To strangle a white man
Slowly
And get away with it

THE DARK SIDE OF THE FORCE SMOLDERS

"Why say white?" jumped James Earl Jones
When I asked about an early love.
"We know she's white, but why?"

I had interracial thoughts on my mind,
Run-ins with the law,
Which the 250-pound Jones dismissed as
"Racial public bullshit."

He became a public figure with
The Great White Hope,
The same year another James Earl
Hit the headlines,
Convincing him that whenever he saw
Coretta Scott King
Her eyes glazed and what entered her mind
Was the name, "One name away
From the nuisance of her life."

The man with a size 15 shoe stuttered
His way through boyhood.
Showed his prick to a sick priest
In the backseat of a car

When he was ten.
Never knew his father until he was a man.
His mother was also a ghost.
When he got out of the Army he
Thought he might become an assassin
If racial anger turned into Civil War.
Instead, he funneled his rage
And mastered his voice,
Controlling the fires within
Even after his house and gun collection
Turned to cinder and ash.

After Primal Screaming and other therapies,
This is what he knows:
  That he is a
  Delayed
   f
   u
   s
   e

HOW ARSENIO LEARNED
TO TALK THAT TALK

Arsenio's grandma taught her grandson
How to clean and polish her .38 revolver
When he was just a boy.
Guns were familiar as soda pop
In their Cleveland ghetto home.
Preacher Hall sometimes chased the Mrs
With one when she made the mistake
Of switching the radio from gospel to soul.
Those fights turned the boy into a sleepwalker,
But unlike Lady Macbeth, who wrestled with spots,
Arsenio surprised his parents' rent party
By peeing on the beer in the fridge.
At 16 he borrowed his mother's car
And drove through a segregated neighborhood
Where white boys danced on the car's hood
And fired bricks through the windshield,
Sprinkling glass shards onto his pomaded hair.
All Arsenio could think of was
Getting through the night alive
So he could get back home,

Exchange his mother's car for her .38
And shoot him some bad white folk.
But Mrs Hall wouldn't let him get revenge,
So Arsenio was spared the prison road not taken
To become a constrained television talk show host.

RELIGION

LIAM NEESON WON'T FORGET

Liam Neeson wrote in my copy of
Schindler's List
"Never forget"
And signed it Oskar.
Tom Keneally
One-upped him
Writing
"Never forget to remember"
Signing his own name

NICK NOLTE HAS DIFFICULTY

Nick Nolte has difficulty
With God.
"If God created man
In his own image
What kind of an image
Is God?
If there is a God
I hope he would overlook
That he made me in his image
Because he sure fucked up"

SINCE MEL GIBSON BELIEVES IN HELL

Since Mel Gibson believes in Hell
Sees the Devil having 8 tongues and 4 horns
Thinks Darwin's Theory of Evolution "Bullshit"
You have to wonder
If his wild temper and verbal craziness
Is an actor's preparation
For taking on
The 4-horned 8-tongued Beast
In his hereafter

FOOD

LAUREN BACALL PLAYED IT FAST & LOOSE

Lauren Bacall played it fast & loose
When she offered me a drink
And I said juice.

I switched to beer
When she dropped her jaw
And scolded, "This isn't
A fucking candy store!"

JOAN COLLINS ASKED FOR CAVIAR

Joan Collins asked for caviar
Louis Roederer
And time to change.
The lacquered photos on the walls
Told one story
The face behind the falling makeup
Another
As she tells how she was
Raped and scraped on her climb,
Providing the small potatoes
From which to scoop the
Little black eggs

LILLIAN GISH OFFERED LEMON COOKIES

Lillian Gish wore a white bathrobe
Offered lemonade and
Lemon cookies
Unfavorably comparing
All her directors
To D.W.
Who once stuck her on
A slab of floating ice
And watched as she
Almost went over
A waterf
   a
    l
     l

STEVEN SEAGAL SWALLOWS PILLS

After a long morning of
Shooting guns and
Twisting arms
Steven Seagal sits at a table
In his trailer
Eating candy bars
A three-plate lunch
And a handful of
Papaya enzyme pills
To aid his digestion

HERE'S WHAT I FED CAMERON DIAZ

Here's what I fed Cameron Diaz
When she came to my house
Bagels and lox
Pumpkin soup
Banana nut bread
Chocolate biscotti

She ate everything
And even washed her plate

THEY CAME LIKE GESTAPO FOR LUCIANO

They came like Gestapo to get Luciano
Pavarotti
Out of my house
These zoot-suited record executives
On album-signing schedules

But Luciano liked the Chinese tacos
Rice balls and sushi
So told the worried eyes to
Let him swallow, the lines
Will only get longer

They paced, made calls,
Wondered what he was doing
In this canyon house
Muttering how hard it had been
To find him

But Luciano liked the chicken
Salad and mini-shrimp dumplings
And stayed awhile
Entertained by my daughter's
Tricycle tricks

Before changing shirts
Exposing moo shoo layers of
Grand opera chest

Finally following his Gestapo
Into the mile-long limo
To face the music

WEED

GRACE JONES BROUGHT A JOINT

Grace Jones brought a joint
Drank champagne
And wore nothing beneath
The silk
That settled on her body
Like the smoke she inhaled

CHEECH & CHONG CAUGHT THE TAIL END

Cheech & Chong caught the tail end
Of a rainbow
Feeling O so regal
While still illegal

MONTEL WILLIAMS WANTED A BOOK

Montel Williams wanted a book that was saleable
He called to ask if I'd be available
To help him write *Climbing Higher*
About the disease he shared with Richard Pryor.
For my services there was one condition
He wanted to address today's Prohibition.
"In my book," he said, "I wanna
Talk about medical marijuana.
I tried Percocet, Vicodin and OxyContin
They fuzzed my brain, I just felt rotten."
But there was one that gave him hope
A dry green weed that some call dope.
When MS made his left foot burn
Dope relieved that sad concern.
So why not legalize that magic weed
And give sick people what they need?

RODNEY DANGERFIELD'S NO RESPECT

Rodney Dangerfield's No Respect
Went all the way back to when he was
Five-year-old Jacob Cohen,
Being paid nickels to kiss old men.
He got No Respect as Jack Roy,
Driving fish and laundry trucks,
Being a singing waiter, and selling
Aluminum siding
Until his third name change
Landed him on the *Ed Sullivan Show.*
No Respect again when Ed Sullivan
Threw him off.
He got No Respect from a dozen therapists
Who couldn't medicate his depression
Until he turned 75 and discovered Wellbutrin.
No wonder he greeted guests
In his open bathrobe, flashing his penis
And taking hits off his dope pipe,
Aware of the irony
Of being a comedian
In an unfunny world

GAMBLING

MARLON IN TAHITI

Hidden in his palm-thatched hut
Marlon Brando
Comes late for dinner
Asking if the hollowed log was
Struck.
Smiling in victory to his young
Secretary who,
Having lost their bet,
Stands on the wooden table
Rubbing her stomach,
Patting her head,
Singing "Somewhere Over the
Rainbow"

GEORGE HAMILTON TURNED FIVE ACES

George Hamilton, balancing a bimbo on his knee
Turned five Aces
The first time he played with us
And smiled like a gentleman
When he beat my five Jacks

FISHER STEVENS JUMPED AT EVERY NOISE

Fisher Stevens snuck us into
Michelle Pfeiffer's house
Wanting to host one poker night
Without her knowing.
He jumped, though, at every noise
And call, afraid she'd return
And find us at her table.
"I'm not whipped," Fisher assured us.
It's just that he knew
If she appeared
He might lose
Every man's fantasy.
Instead, he only lost
His money

HARRY DEAN STANTON BROUGHT HIS SOLITAIRE DECK

Harry Dean Stanton brought his Solitaire deck
Called Texas Hold'em table stakes
Kept the betting high
Then turned his pairs
Looking at a straight

RANDY QUAID TRIPPED DOWN DIANE KEATON'S STEPS

Randy Quaid came half hour late
Then tripped down Diane Keaton's steps
As we sat playing high-low wild card
Poker
Wanting to know
Whether to deal him in

DIANE KEATON TOOK A BEATIN'

Diane Keaton took a beatin'
Playing poker without cheatin'
Exclaimed at least a dozen "Fucks"
As she won, then lost, forty bucks
A week later she was so miffed she
Doubled her curses
But still dropped fifty

JIMMY-THE-MOUTH WOODS

Jimmy-the-Mouth Woods
Came to play poker—
Said he knew all the games—
But being a compulsive talker
Couldn't stop the constant
Card commentary.
By midnight this babbling
Jabberwocky had exhausted us.
When he said how much
Fun he was having
And what a swell group of guys
We were, we held our side glances
In check, though raised the bet
On his future
In our game

SPORTS

FORE!

After Jeff Daniels broke 70
He traded his clubs
For a guitar.
He knew he'd have to
Find a pro and
Play twice a week
To get any better
So chose instead
To learn the Blues

MICKEY MANTLE SITS AT A TABLE

Mickey Mantle sits at a table
In Brentano's in Beverly Hills
Signing books not baseballs
As women past their primes see
Their youths in his eyes
And men say hi
To their dreams

LEW, ABDUL, HE'S OUR MAN!

I went to college with Lew Alcindor
Who, on Pauley Pavilion's floor,
Seemed to ignore us as we roared
Each time his hook or jump shot scored

With Muslim ideas his mind explored
And when he left, Alcindor no more,
Kareem Abdul Jabbar entered hoop lore

BIG LITTLE MAN

I followed Willie Shoemaker
Into the locker room at
Del Mar
Watched him dress and joke
With the other jockeys
This shy small man
Whose hands controlled
The thousands of thoroughbreds
Who ran a little faster
When he rode their backs

The Shoe didn't talk much
What he had to say
Was done on the track
When the gates flew open
And the hooves threw back the dirt

In his bedroom, after
Winning three races he sat on
The floor and remembered
How he once misjudged the
Finish line at the
Kentucky Derby

After his paralyzing accident
I wonder how many of his races
He reruns
And whether he thinks more
About the victories or
The losses

WRITING

MARLON BRANDO WRITES HIS NOVEL

Marlon Brando writes his novel
About Tahiti, pearls, and
Ancient China
And talks on his ham radio
To a man in Florida
Who tells him
How lightning came
Through his phone
Into his ear
Not once
But twice

GEORGE C. SCOTT POURS FROM A PITCHER OF BLOODY MARYS

George C. Scott pours from a pitcher of
Bloody Marys
As he gazes at his wife
Trish trotting on horseback
In their backyard

He swears he'll never read
What he has to say in print
But upstairs in his study
He tries to forget
Holding a broken bottle to
Ava Gardner's face
And how John Huston once
Rode his back to keep him
From striking one more drunken
Blow for manhood
As he scribbles the story of
The Civil War into his notebooks
Filling up volumes of the novels
He may never publish but
Will always read

KATHARINE AFRICAN HEPBURN QUEEN

She sits there, Kate Hepburn,
Hands shaking, neck covered,
Broken foot raised on a stool,
Daring me to defend myself
That no great movies have been
Made from great books.
Au contraire,
Hepburn says,
And often times better

SAUL BELLOW QUITE A FELLOW

When I asked Saul Bellow
About his Nobel Prize
He said he'd give it to Norman Mailer
"If he had anything to trade."
That Saul Bellow, quite a fellow

JAMES A. MICHENER LEAVES NO MARGINS

James A. Michener leaves no margins
In letters, on pages
Because to him
Empty space is
Wasted space
And pregnant pauses
Must be delivered

ALEX HALEY RARELY

Alex Haley rarely
Wrote insincerely
But all that loot
From finding his Roots
Blocked him into eternity

J.P. DONLEAVY AMONG THE DEAD

J.P. Donleavy gripped my Fiat's
Door handle tightly
On the way to Forest Lawn.
He likes to walk among the dead.

In Westwood he stood still
Against a building
And was recognized by an
Irish comedian driving by
Shouting "Mike! Mike!"

Along dank Dickensian
London backstreets
Strangers still snicker
In passing, thinking,
He's sure, of that *Ginger*
Toilet scene
Raining feces on
The poor wife's
Head

YOU CAN JUDGE HIS BOOK BY ITS TITLE

Elmore Leonard goes by Dutch
   Prefers one-word titles
Like *Stick*, *Glitz*, and *Touch*.
   And when he finds one word too few
He doubles them from one to two.
   Get Shorty's fine; *Rum Punch* the same
But sometimes Dutch adds a *The* to the name.
   The Big Bounce was rejected 84 times,
The Moonshine War had little crime.
   The ones that seem to work the best
Are one- and two-word titles, more or less.
   He must have known that when he was done
With *Thirty-Nine Lashes*, a Western
   He changed to *Forty Lashes Less One*.
If he couldn't make it less than three,
   He went for four, *freaky deaky*!

THE MAN FROM BLOOMFIELD VILLAGE

If Elmore Leonard committed a crime
He wouldn't go where the money is
Like Willie Sutton did
But where his neighbors live.
During a party he'd crash
Taking their jewels and cash
Then return to his den
Where he penned *LaBrava* and *Touch*
And write another, this doppelDutch

SALAD DRESSING

Sing a song of Joyce Carol Oates
Working on another book
When comes an invitation
That requires that she cook

The pot-luck dinner spared her
From dishing a main meal
Instead they asked for salad
Which her friends thought no big deal

But after a day's writing
About the sex life of a man
The kitchen was as alien
As reviews without a pan

Her mind was on her work
(A thousand pages of notes were done);
Cutting greens wasn't a priority
With the book stuck on page 81

It only occurred to her at the car
That something was missing—
Could it be a jar
Of salad dressing?

"Am I supposed to make that, too?"
She asked her husband Ray
"I think you should," he said,
 In his quiet polite way

So Joyce the writer went back
To fill a tumbler to the brim
With vinegar, herbs and spices
Then went out to the car again

This time fretting that the
Liquid might spill
As thcy drove the back roads
In the evening Princeton chill

Ray reduced her anxieties
By making sure the lid was secure
Joyce returned to her man's thoughts
Of ejaculations premature

YOU COULDN'T MISS GAY TALESE

You couldn't miss Gay Talese's sharp look
At the UCLA Festival of Books
Splendid in tailored suit & vest
White collared pink shirt & yellow tie no less
Topped with a black banded white Borsalino hat
A throwback to when writers dressed like that

In town to promote his new memoir
Which the *N.Y. Times* felt under par
Calling it "more hodgepodge than collage"
A nasty piece of reportage
It put him in a state of despair
Kurt Andersen's review seemed so unfair

When I invited him to see Al Pacino in *Salome*
He recalled Pacino doing it with Marisa Tomei
He'd go if I agreed to change into a tie & jacket
I said I didn't think I could hack it
"It's L.A., we're casual," I said in dismay
(Besides, my clothes were at home, 12 miles away)
"Al would be shocked to see me so dressed"
"Don't do it for Al, but for me," Gay said,
Still distressed

PENELOPE CRUZ NOTHING TO LOSE

Penelope Cruz
Nothing to lose
Said "Let's go sit over there"
Where Gore Vidal was lunching
At the Chateau Marmont
She wanted to overhear
His conversation with
TV Cop & conspiracy theorist
Richard Belzer

She didn't know Gore
But when I told her
He was a great American writer
She thought eavesdropping
Was worth a shot

But the maitre d'
Couldn't get us close
So we had to settle near
Jerry Stiller's son
Ben, the funny Focker
Who came to say hello
And pet her dog Vino

Who sniffed his crotch
As Ben glanced at his watch
Rolled his eyes, and said "Very cute"
Which left the three of us mute
An opportunity missed
For a humorous twist

The remark didn't quite fit
What could have revealed Ben's wit
And left us wondering
What the soon-to-be-departed
Vidal might have quipped

INTERVIEWING

I'D LIKE TO SAY I HAD A BALL

I'd like to say I had a ball
Interviewing Jake Gyllenhaal;
Sadly, I did not
When his publicist said "20 minutes is all you've got."
What gall, this Gyllenhaal!
Who wouldn't garner my affection
If he truly needed such protection.
There were things, of course, to make inquiry:
His divorced parents; his sister Maggie;
The *Nine Stories* of J.D. Salinger;
The death of costar Heath Ledger.
Reading, for him, was a great distress
Until he became Salinger obsessed.
As for Heath, his *Brokeback* passion,
"That's between us," was all he'd ration.
His family—sister, father, mother—
"Conflicts, definitely; people pushing each other."
They told him movies were their life's drama;
Mom's was *Jules and Jim*, Dad *La Strada*.
Three things I learned from this half-Jew:

"There's always calculation in the things I do."
"I'm not afraid of the darkness"—so brave.
"Accepting what you have is what you have."
When I said I had a problem with that
He laughed as he sipped from his coffee cup.
"Of course you do; your 20 minutes are up"

BOBBY DE NIRO BOBS & WEAVES

Bobby De Niro bobs & weaves
Dodging questions like fists
Thrown at his head
Stammering in unfinished sentences
While picking at a scab on his
Cheek.
Turning off the tape recorder to say
He never liked Bogart
Leaving blood on the machine

GOV. JESSE VENTURA CAME TO DINNER

Gov. Jesse Ventura came to dinner
With his wife Terry and son Tyrel
Six months after our interview
Lowered his popularity by 20%.
We were both caught by surprise
In a media frenzy
After the Governor of Minnesota
Called organized religion "a sham
And a crutch for weak-minded people,"
Thought a naval sexual scandal
Much ado about nothing,
And wished to be reincarnated as a
38 DD bra

His Secret Service checked out
Our Hollywood Hills house
The day before this former wrestler
Who wore feathered boas into the ring
Arrived.
"I don't know why we're here, I
Hated your interview" his wife Terry said

But Jesse wanted to meet Oliver Stone
Whose conspiratorial *JFK* made him
The governor's hero
And I arranged for Stone and
Robert Towne to join us

The governor brought wine
We smoked cigars
And could all agree
The food was delicious

I'D RATHER BE ALONE, SHARON STONE

I'd rather be alone
Than spend another day with Sharon Stone.
Got her to tattle
About her losing custody battle
To ex-husband Phil–
A bitter pill.
"With that guy, I was conned."
To which I thought, Oh come on!
You're the one who put him
In a cage with a komodo dragon.

But though I left, we weren't done;
In fact, she felt we hadn't begun.
At the photo shoot
She asked to reboot
To an editor she sequestered.
I'd like a do-over, she requested.
And in short order
She got another reporter.
The interview was no longer mine;
Instead, they offered a shared by-line

This custody battle Sharon won
Which, simply put, left me stunned,
And though I profiled her in the past
This time with her would be my last.
Yes, I'd rather be alone
Than spend another day with Sharon Stone

BOB KNIGHT FINISHED HIS FOOD

Bob Knight finished his food
Before mine arrived and
Didn't want to wait

This was before he threatened
To throw me out of his car
Because he didn't like my questions

Before his head nearly exploded
When I refused to hand over my tapes
And he punched me in the gut

Before I would flee from my hotel
To catch an early flight out of
Indiana

Before all this
I should have known

BARBARA WALTERS FLUTTERED HER LIDS

Barbara Walters fluttered her lids
Refusing to answer any
Questions about face lifts
While her publicist shouted
"That's not fair!"
Quite forgetting what this
Game is all about

SCENES

MAE WEST ALWAYS MADE AN ENTRANCE

Mae West always made an entrance
Even when exiting

DOLLY PARTON AT 3:00 A.M.

Dolly Parton at 3:00 a.m.
Orders fruits and cheeses
Pats the motel mattress
And listens to my African ghost stories
As I fight off dizzying thoughts
Of what that pat meant

BETTE CALLING

Bette Midler called
To say she shouldn't have said
What she thought she said
About being funnier than
Madonna
Asking to put it off-the-record
When she hadn't put it on

BARBRA STREISAND WANTS TO GET IT RIGHT

Barbra Streisand wants to get it right.
The pool tiles
To the uneducated eye
All seem the same
But the color she's looking for
Is neither gray nor black
And so she puts each in a
Bucket of chlorine water
And considers.
Because if she chooses wrong
She'll have to drain the pool
And do it a third time.
It's summer—a hard time
To be without a pool
In Malibu

ELLIOTT GOULD SAID TO ELVIS PRESLEY

Elliott Gould said to Elvis Presley
"I may be crazy, but
What's that gun doing
Sitting on *your* hip?"

AMERICA THE BOO! TIFUL

America, to Sir Anthony Hopkins,
Is like an Ayn Rand novel,
An acid-less acid trip
Which he discovered
When he crossed it—
From Mormon Salt Lake City
To cowboy Santa Fe,
Death-of-a-president Dallas
To Cajun Baton Rouge,
Southern drawl Savannah
To his glass cell in Pittsburgh—
Driving alone,
Listening to Handel's "Messiah,"
Rehearsing how he'd play
The cannibal Hannibal Lecter.
It was the voice that came to him,
The greased-back hair,
The tailored dental white uniform,
As he traveled the roads
And slept in *Last Picture Show* motels,
Seeing Jodie Foster in his dreams
Wondering how she'd taste

I CAPTURED AL PACINO

I captured Al Pacino
Framed in the rectangle of
Wire fence
As he pushed a wet broom
Across the paddle tennis court
Sweeping rain water
Before we played

FUNNY MONEY

Jack Nicholson keeps torn up money
In a glass ashtray in his
Living room
What the hell is *that*
About?

ORANGE COUNTY SUTRA

Allen Ginsberg had never been
In a limousine;
Rearranged the books behind him
At the Laguna book store so
Only his were in the picture;
Kissed me on the lips goodbye
At John Wayne airport
In front of shocked travelers
Going on his flight

BETTY FRIEDAN GOT UP TO LEAVE

Betty Friedan got up to leave
During our cable TV conversation.
She said she just couldn't believe
The insulting nature of my interrogation

Like what she thought of Phyllis Schlafly?
And why Ms instead of Miss?
She didn't bother responding affably
Just ripped off her mic with "I don't need this!"

"Betty, please, sit down, let's finish"
I said trying to keep her in her seat
And ease her fear of being diminished
This mother of *The Feminine Mystique*

14 CARAT GOLDIE

Goldie Hawn was cool as ice
When a stranger kneeled
By our table at Katsu's Third
And made like he knew her.
When she didn't introduce him
I thought she had forgotten
His name.
He spoke with dreams in his
Eyes, invited her to sail.
She acted as if they were friends,
Reducing an embarrassment
To just another moment
In a star's life.
Though I'm sure she was thinking
Uncute thoughts
Because Goldie can be tough as
Broken glass
When she isn't cool as ice

I KISSED FARRAH FAWCETT

On a dark night off Coldwater Canyon
A blonde driver was looking for direction.
I stopped my car, got out
And asked if I could help.
"I'm lost," she said.
I recognized her voice.
"Farrah? Is that you?"
We hadn't seen each other in years
But she remembered our
Paddle tennis games.
When she got straightened out
She gave me her number
And a friendly kiss

Farrah Fawcett had
Very soft lips

SYLVESTER STALLONE FLINCHED

Sylvester Stallone flinched
When I snapped my mic
And lunged at him
To keep the 30-foot sun screen
From falling on his
Carefully coiffed head

GEEZ ROY, SAY CHEESE

Roy Clark had no spark
When we spoke backstage
In Vegas

Hiromi was with me
Posing as my photographer
Though she had no idea
How to use the camera

It didn't matter, since it,
Like Roy,
Wasn't loaded

SHELLEY WINTERS SEES MARLON BRANDO

Shelley Winters sees Marlon Brando
Jogging the hills by her home.
Do such folk
Remember those youthful New York
Winter nights
When the only heat came from
Their bodies
And life still had passion?

I DROVE ANGELINA'S CAR

The rainy night before Angelina Jolie
Changed her life
Leaving Billy Bob behind
To venture off to Sierra Leone
As a U.N. Goodwill Ambassador
She came to my house
And talked for hours…
About the great love she had
For the man she was about to leave
("If Billy was a woman, I'd be a lesbian")
About the closeness to her father Jon
Who was about to become a stranger
("We are a lot alike. We can push each
other's buttons")
About personal violence
("S&M was a need")
About that kiss with her
Brother at the Oscar's
("A lot of people kiss on the mouth")
About her favorite artist Egon Schiele
("He draws naked, exposed women
looking right at you")
Her knife collection

("All in a locked case")
And tattoos
("A statement of who you are")
But what I remember most
Was backing her SUV
From my driveway
Into my car
On the other side
Of the wet street

BRUCE SPRINGSTEEN GETS REJECTED

Bruce Springsteen sees
Al Pacino at Chianti's
And wanders by—to join us?
Pacino very nonplussed
Says "These are my friends"
A subtle message sent

Bruce was with his girl Patti
This before they would marry
They stood there waiting to be asked to sit
Bruce knew Al, once gave him his E Street jacket

It sure would have been fun
To hang with the rocker Born to Run
But no invite was extended
Springsteen left, I'm sure offended

But it was really our loss
When Al pulled rank on The Boss

THE JOKING DR. FEYNMAN

Richard Feynman, quantum leaper,
Kissed his Muse and tried to keep her.
Pondered quarks, black holes
And matters physic,
As he thought
In meters rhythmic

Solved the mystery
Of the Shuttle explosion
By dipping an O-ring
Into water frozen

In things atomic he had a post;
Picked the locks at Los Alamos.
His work was often in defiance,
He won a Nobel for his science

Enjoyed women, married thrice.
Sketching nudes was his vice.
Played the bongos, loved to teach
Studied languages out of reach

Shopping once, he stopped a fall
Though hit his head against a wall.
To alleviate pressure from his brain
They drilled two holes and let it drain

In his best-seller he confessed
How as a youth he was possessed
With radios, microscopes, puzzles, cars
And topless girls in funky bars

For a man who was a genius
Dr. Feynman had
An active penis

HEY! HEY! LBJ!

I almost killed Lyndon Johnson
In Atlantic City.
I was randomly chosen
To help carry a giant swing
With a seated wooden cowgirl
Into the convention
As the band played "Happy Days
Are Here Again."
But when we reached the podium
The swing began to sway
And nearly toppled on
The president's beaming face.
Had that happened
Vietnam might have been over
Before the Tet offensive,
And Robert Kennedy
Would be alive today

A GOOD LIFE

BILLY DEE WILLIAMS BLUSHES INVISIBLY

Billy Dee Williams blushes invisibly
Remembering those gigolo days
And whorehouse nights
Knowing when it was good
And O so very
Bad

WALKEN'S TALKIN'

Chris Walken's not just talkin'
He's making me a pot of tea
Offering artichokes in virgin oil
And leftover mini-Crunch Halloween bars

"I don't mind being called spooky"
He says "but creepy bothers me
Creepy is like an insect
It has no spine"

Chris has a dish towel
Which he uses to wipe tea cup
Moisture from his
Spotless kitchen countertop
He doesn't like mess
Or to be messed with
This alien from the
Planet Show Biz

Performing now for half a century
As he celebrates his 53rd birthday
His orange hair brushed
Pompadour high

The crow lines by his eyes
Lengthening down his cheeks
His skin the color of vampire ghoul

This lover of porn and Presley
Of Jerry Lewis & John Wayne
This creepy crawly spooky actor
Who goes for the head when he shoots
And slays 'em at least half the time

Not bad for an actor
Still in his prime

HUGH HEFNER TOOK ME INTO HIS BEDROOM

Hugh Hefner took me into his bedroom
To show off his toys
Then out to the rolling gardens
To look at birds, feed the koi
And let the woolly monkey grab
My ankle

In the future, he hoped to be
More highly esteemed
Because his life has been
"A wonderful tale;
I'm glad it happened
To me"

SAYONARA

I COULDN'T SEE JOSH LOGAN

I couldn't see Josh Logan
Who sat on his living room
Couch, so small and frail,
As if the furniture was
Swallowing him.
I couldn't hear him when
He spoke,
But listened politely,
Asking questions, stirring memories
Of a man still breathing
But *sayonara*

I LOVE LUCY DOESN'T LOVE LIFE

I Love Lucy doesn't love life.
Didn't think funny
Never ad-libbed.
The Marx Bros scared her
The 3 Stooges doused her
Busby Berkeley was too drunk
To notice her.
She once threw coffee on
Katharine Hepburn
But never apologized because
Buster Keaton taught her to be
Prop proud.
Cursed death which took her friends
And went willingly because
Surprise!
I Love Lucy didn't love life

THE LAST CLOWN

Robin William's suicide was a blow
My initial reaction: No way to go!
Our comic alien forgot his part
For all who loved his warm giant heart

A model for comics known
and upcoming
His heroes were Winters, Einstein,
and Hawking

He sought to be thought
The Benevolent Fool
But he also became
Our own treasured jewel

He saw the world the way it was
A circus in chaos seen from afar
His role, he said, with a thoughtful pause
"The last clown out of that little car"

One late night, when my car wouldn't start
He rolled up his sleeves to help me depart
Pushing and sweating, all with great zeal
As I held onto the steering wheel

I waved goodbye when the motor kicked in
In the rearview mirror—my last sight of him

MENTORS

Five men in different fields
At different times
Pointed the way to living
A fulfilling life

John Huston said to do good work
Arthur Singer to use the best materials
Jan de Swart to do what you want to do
Enrique Cortes to keep on doing it
And Ted Harris to ignore those
Who get in the way

Two of them are buried in New York
Two in California
Enrique's still there
To see if I listened

Lawrence Grobel (www.lawrencegrobel.com) has written 22 books and for numerous national magazines and newspapers, including the *New York Times, Newsday, Rolling Stone, Entertainment Weekly, Reader's Digest, American Way, Parade, Details, TV Guide, Redbook, Cosmopolitan, Penthouse, Diversion, Writer's Digest, The Saturday Evening Post,* and *AARP.* He has been a contributing editor at *Playboy, Movieline, Hollywood Life, Autograph,* New Zealand's *World,* Bulgaria's *Ego,* and Poland's *Trendy* magazines. Between 1968-71 he taught in the Peace Corps at the Ghana Institute of Journalism. He created the MFA in Professional Writing program for Antioch University in 1977 and served as its Director for three years. In 1981 he received a National Endowment for the Arts grant for fiction. His *Conversations with Capote* received a PEN Special Achievement award and reached the top of several bestseller lists. His book on Al Pacino was awarded the Prix Literraire from the French Society of film critics. From 2001—2011 he taught in the English Dept. at UCLA. He appeared as himself in Al Pacino's *Wilde Salome* and the documentary *Salinger.* He is married to artist Hiromi Oda and they have two daughters, Maya and Hana.

COMMANDO EX

An excerpt in verse from the novella by

Lawrence Grobel

A Rip-Roaring Freewheeling Thrill Seeker Humpin'
& Bumpin' His Way across Africa

Prologue

Let's not do this slow, no,
let's get the words out fast, yes,
steam through the history, gas, pass,
Commando Ex got class, crass?
Here comes, hold it now,
the rise and droppings, the stiffenings and
   squirtings,
the balls-and-jacks beginnings of a never-ending
 life-suspending continent-hopping mind-expanding
experience-stretching story: the life and times,
the lays and plays, the huck and suck
of an antsy chancy ice cream cone of a fella;
a dope-smoking, seed-choking, penis-poking free-
   dom flighter,
wronged and righter, cycle rider, self-propelled glider.
So...bang your horn, blow your drum,
drip your cum and armchair his fun...
for the whirl and curl of it, the hop skip and jump
   of it,
the fantasizing fun of it, the jocular joy of it.
Let's leave truth and exaggeration behind,
get into the smash bang crunch of this singular

demolition derby of a guy, a liver, a lover, a kisser,
   a hugger...
a grabber of balls, squeezer of twats, teaser of
   cultures,
a galactic whirlwind of a self-proclaimed Commando,
the one, the only, the visa-defying terrifying
moan and sighing Ex
travagant, uberant, pedocious, traordinary, treme,
   orbitant...
ah, yes...actly!

Look, now, at this backpacking, hulk strapping,
bone cracking fellow, fresh from a river bath,
as French-speaking Africans steal silent eyefuls
of this copper body, heavy dong swinging,
balls hanging like turkey eggs, elephant leathery—
a wide-chested sculpted Adonis,
blue eyed sandy haired, Australian accented,
glistening wet sweat of a boy-man
who just jumped the river on his 700cc Moto Guzzi
   motorcycle
as lazed fishermen popped their eyeballs into their
   nets as he soared.
Nothing like some morning action to wake up
   the day.

Hey! What's the Commando doing in Africa?
Last seen tucking a Coca-Cola under his belt and
showering the sand of the Spanish Sahara
on both sides of his bellowing machine

as he streamed across the desert single-handed
and multi-purposed,
here he now pops at the river Niger
washing out the scratchy Sahara sand and
doing a little of his showing off to get the natives
whispering
and to keep from any hassling. Because no one likes
to bother a man on a roaring mutha of a bike
which churns sand, earth, road and air at devilish
speeds,
no, sir, even the law is wary of starting with a man
possessed,
because here in Africa, any man who does what
Ex just did
has got to be a little wacko in the upstairs...
and you don't fuck around with a crazy,
not while there're spirits watching.
And did you see the size of his lance, by chance?
Did you get a glance at his glans?
Bring on the womenfolk, let's see how he can poke,
throw him a J to smoke, Commando's set to start
a cult.
Eeeee, how long can this go on?

Other Books By Lawrence Grobel

CATCH A FALLEN STAR (a novel)

Catch a Fallen Star is the story of actor Layton Cross, a man who fails upward, as he touches all bases: drugs, divorce, violence, megalomania. We're privy to all the sordid events: his public battles with his ex-wives; his clash with the head of a major studio; his best friend's deceit; and his daughter's troubling secret.

BEGIN AGAIN FINNEGAN (a novel)

How far would you go to help your best friend? That's the question journalist Devin Hunter faces when movie star Adrian Kiel asks him to be his alibi to cover a possible murder. Devin's decision starts a chain of events that spiral out of control as he tries to hold the pieces of his life together. This is a story about secret lives, psychiatric wards, celebrity "justice," blackmail, betrayal and a modern day take on James Joyce in exile; but mostly it's about relationships and their consequences. It explores the loyalty of a friendship that increasingly appears one-sided and slowly implodes.

THE BLACK EYES OF AKBAH (a novella)

After leaving Ghana, where they served for two years in the Peace Corps, Eric and Anika agree to travel together to Kenya and India to get to know each other better and see if they want to spend the rest of their lives together. They agree to work their way across the Indian Ocean on a cargo ship ominously called The Black Eyes of Akbah. The crew is a melting pot of all the indigenous peoples of the region. The chilling terror that happens along the way will change the way they see each other and the world they thought they knew. Oliver Stone compared this story to a cross between *The African Queen* and *Midnight Express.*

COMMANDO EX (a novella)

Commando Ex is a wild Australian hedonist racing across Africa on his Moto Guzzi motorcycle, chasing thrills and adventure, living life to the max and flaunting what you can be if you're absolutely free. "So keep up, speed along, trip flip and skip through the one life worth living, the fully explored, high geared unfeared not scared life of the Commando. Sight...on!"

THE HUSTONS

When John Huston died at 81 on August 28, 1987, America lost a towering figure in movie history. The director of such classic films as *The Treasure of the Sierra Madre, The African Queen, The Maltese Falcon, Prizzi's Honor,* and *The Dead,* John Huston evoked passionate responses from everyone he encountered. He was at the center of a dynasty, with three generations of Oscar winners (Walter, John and Anjelica). Now the complete story of this remarkable family is told in *The Hustons.* The book chronicles the family's history—from Walter's days on the vaudeville circuit and his later fame on Broadway, through John's meteoric rise, to Anjelica's and Danny's emergence as formidable actors in film today.

CONVERSATIONS WITH CAPOTE

Six months after Truman Capote died in 1984, *Conversations with Capote* was published and reached the top of best-seller lists in both New York and San Francisco. Said the *San Francisco Chronicle*, "All the rumors you ever heard about Capote are here… Refreshing …thoughtful and reflective." Grobel talked to Capote over a period of two years and it remains an essential part of the Capote canon.

CONVERSATIONS WITH BRANDO

Playboy named Lawrence Grobel "The Interviewer's Interviewer" for his uncanny ability to get America's greatest and most reclusive actor, Marlon Brando, to speak openly for the first time. When Grobel expanded the interview into a book, *American Cinematographer* said it "penetrates the complex nature of a very private man, probing his feelings on women and sex, Native Americans, corporate America and the FBI." James A. Michener thought it "explained Brando accurately:

the torment, the arrogance—almost willed towards self-destruction—but above all, the soaring talent."

CONVERSATIONS WITH MICHENER

After successfully publishing his book-length interviews with Truman Capote and Marlon Brando, Grobel approached author James A. Michener as his next subject, and wound up taping their discussions over a 17 year period, right up until the last week of Michener's life. The result is the most comprehensive of all Grobel's "Conversation" books. Michener, who didn't start writing novels until he was 40, was a true citizen of the world. He foresaw the future of countries as diverse as Afghanistan, Poland, Japan, Spain, Hungary, Mexico, Israel, and the U.S. His books—like *Hawaii, The Source, Iberia, Sayonara,* and *Tales of the South Pacific*–sold millions of copies and many were made into films or TV miniseries. *Conversations with Michener* is as relevant today as it was prescient when it first appeared in 1999.

CONVERSATIONS WITH AVA GARDNER

Ava Gardner had an aversion to reporters and their tape recorders, but when she felt at ease she didn't hold back. It was just a matter of finding the right person to make her feel comfortable. Two years before she died, she asked Lawrence Grobel to work with her on her memoir. In this series of candid conversations, the reclusive actress opens up about her three volatile marriages to Mickey Rooney, Artie

Shaw and Frank Sinatra; about Howard Hughes' 15-year pursuit of her; and reveals how George C. Scott was so crazily in love with her that he attacked her on three occasions. She talks about her tomboy childhood as a tobacco farmer's daughter in North Carolina and how she was "discovered" and became a contract player at MGM. She is forthright about her friendships with Hemingway, Dominguin, and Brando, and explains why John Huston was her favorite director. She admits to her struggles with alcohol and speaks intimately about the debilitating stroke she suffered toward the end of her life.

AL PACINO in Conversation with Lawrence Grobel

For more than a quarter century, Al Pacino has spoken freely and deeply with Lawrence Grobel on subjects as diverse as childhood, acting, and fatherhood. Here are the complete conversations and shared observations between the actor and the writer; the result is an intimate and revealing look at one of the most accomplished, and private, artists in the world.

"I WANT YOU IN MY MOVIE!"
My Acting Debut & Other Misadventures Filming Al Pacino's *Wilde Salome*

"Why *am* I doing this?" Al Pacino wondered a year into his personal movie about his obsession with *Salome,* Oscar Wilde's lyrical play, written in 1891. "No one saw *Looking for Richard*, who's going to want to see something about Oscar Wilde?" In *"I Want You in My Movie!"* Grobel found the answer to that question and more when he joined the crew and followed the creative process of filmmaking from inception to completion. His meticulous journal is as close to being there as a reader can ever hope to get, offering an intimate peek behind the curtain, documenting the hopes, dreams, frustrations and complexities of Pacino and all the people who come in and out of his life.

THE ART OF THE INTERVIEW: Lessons from a Master of the Craft

Joyce Carol Oates called Lawrence Grobel "The Mozart of Interviewers." J.P. Donleavy wrote, "Grobel is the most intelligent interviewer in the United States." In *The Art of the Interview*, Grobel reveals the most memorable stories from his career, along with examples of the most candid moments from his long list of famous interviewees, from Oscar-winning actors and Nobel laureates to Pulitzer Prize-winning writers and sports figures.

SIGNING IN: 50 Celebrity Profiles

From 2005—2010 Lawrence Grobel wrote over 50 magazine articles about his in-depth encounters with some of the most famous people in the world. Each piece had only one caveat: to include at least a paragraph about something the celebrity had signed. So Grobel built each portrait around a signed photo, poster, drawing, personal letter, or book inscription, many of which are shown in this engaging book. Among the entertainers and writers included are Barbra Streisand, Marlon Brando, Al Pacino, Farrah Fawcett, Henry Fonda, Madonna, Angelina Jolie, Robin Williams, Steve Martin, Luciano Pavarotti, Anthony Kiedis, Truman Capote, Monica Lewinsky, Norman Mailer, Elmore Leonard, and Saul Bellow.

ICONS

When the editors of *Trendy* magazine in Poland asked Lawrence Grobel to write detailed cover stories about some of the Hollywood icons he's known over the years, Grobel took the opportunity to profile fifteen internationally beloved stars: Jack Nicholson, Angelina Jolie, Halle Berry, Anthony Hopkins, Kim Basinger, Anthony Kiedis, Jodie Foster, Nicole Kidman, Meryl Streep, Gwyneth Paltrow, Cameron Diaz, Tom Waits, Penelope Cruz, Sharon Stone, and Robert De Niro.

YOU SHOW ME YOURS: A Memoir

Lawrence Grobel's energetic memoir begins with him growing up on the streets of Brooklyn, where he was nearly kidnapped as an infant, and the suburbs of Long Island, where his sex education began at a very early age. By the age of 15, he was competing with his best friend over a modern day Lolita. In 1967 he marched with Dr. Martin Luther King Jr. in Mississippi under a hail of bullets, and came of age under the guidance of an enlightened Mexican Don Juan. After graduating from UCLA, he joined the Peace Corps, which afforded him the chance to communicate with a fetish high priestess in Ghana, pygmies in Uganda, and stoned-out hippies on the island of Lamu. In the '70s he became a New Journalist. When he left New York for California he turned his skills to celebrity interviews. It's a journey through the Looking Glass of American Culture from the post-War '50s, the sexually liberated '60s, the Civil Rights movement, and the "Me Decade."

ABOVE THE LINE: Conversations About the Movies

Above the Line is a dazzling gathering of insights and anecdotes from all corners of the film industry—interviews that reveal the skills, intelligence, experiences, and emotions of eleven key players who produce, write, direct, act in, and review the movies: Oliver Stone, Anthony Hopkins, Jodie Foster, Robert Evans, Lily Tomlin, Jean-Claude Van Damme, Harrison Ford, Robert Towne, Sharon Stone, and Siskel and Ebert.

ENDANGERED SPECIES: Writers Talk about Their Craft, Their Visions, Their Lives

Norman Mailer once told Lawrence Grobel that writers may be an endangered species. And Saul Bellow told him, "The country has changed so, that what I do no longer signifies anything, as it did when I was young." But to judge from this collection, writers and writing aren't done for quite yet. Sometimes serious, sometimes funny, sometimes caustic, always passionate, the twelve writers in

Endangered Species (Bellow, Mailer, Ray Bradbury, J.P. Donleavy, James Ellroy, Allen Ginsberg, Andrew Greeley, Alex Haley, Joseph Heller, Elmore Leonard, Joyce Carol Oates, and Neil Simon) memorably state their case for what they do and how they do it.

CONVERSATIONS WITH ROBERT EVANS

"I don't want to have a slow death," Robert Evans told Lawrence Grobel. "That's my fear. I've had a gun put in my mouth, a gun put at my temple. I've had a gun put on me five different times to talk, and not once have I ever talked." But talk is what Evans does in his conversations with Grobel. As the head of Paramount Studios in the 1970s Evans produced some of the most iconic movies of that era, including *Love Story, The Odd Couple, Paper Moon, True Grit, Catch 22, Chinatown,* and *The Godfather.* But his life was much more than that of a movie producer and this book is eye-opening in its honesty and its finger-pointing.

CLIMBING HIGHER

A New York Times Bestseller, *Climbing Higher* is the story of Montel Williams' life and personal struggles with MS. In 1999, after almost 20 years of mysterious symptoms that he tried to ignore, Montel Williams, a decorated former naval intelligence officer and Emmy Award-winning talk show host, was finally diagnosed with multiple sclerosis. Like others suffering from the devastating and often disabling disease, which attacks the central nervous system, Montel was struck with denial, fear, depression, and anger. Yet somehow he emerged with a fierce determination not to be beaten down by MS, and to live the most vital and productive life possible while becoming a dedicated spokesperson for the disease. In addition, with the help of a team of leading doctors, *Climbing Higher* offers up-to-the-minute information on new MS research and invaluable guidance for managing MS.

MARILYN & ME

In 1960 and 1962 Lawrence Schiller was asked by *Paris Match* and *Life* magazines to photograph Marilyn Monroe on the set of *Let's Make Love* and *Something's Got to Give*, which was never completed because of her controversial death. Schiller had befriended Monroe and he asked Lawrence Grobel to help him shape the story of that friendship into this memoir. It's a new addition to the Monroe saga from the perspective of an impressionistic young photographer and the iconic sex symbol.

Yoga? No! SHMOGA!

Google "Yoga" and 103,000,000 items come up. One hundred and three *million*! Yet for everyone who practices yoga, there are dozens of others who just sit and watch. *Yoga? No! Shmoga!* is for those who sit and watch, as well as for those who actually do yoga and have a sense of humor. In 43 short chapters it pokes fun at sports, religion, exercise, Wall Street, art, entertainment, and people looking for an excuse to not do anything more than lift a finger.

Made in the USA
Las Vegas, NV
21 January 2023

66012521R00143